Christmas Sweet Treats

BARRON'S

First edition for the United States and Canada published by Barron's Educational Series, Inc.

All inquiries should be addressed to:
Barron's Educational Series, Inc.
250 Wireless Boulevard
Hauppauge, New York 11788
www.barronseduc.com
ISBN: 978-0-7641-6558-0
Library of Congress Catalog Card No. 2012930672
Printed in China
9 8 7 6 5 4 3 2 1

Contents

Cooking Equipment

Before you begin to get creative in the kitchen, it's a good idea to take a look through the drawers and cupboards to make sure you have the cooking equipment you will need.

• To complete the recipes in this book, you will need to use a selection of everyday cooking equipment and utensils, such as mixing bowls, saucepans, a sifter, a wire rack, paper towels, knives, spoons, forks and a cutting board.

• Of course, you'll need to weigh and measure the ingredients, so you'll need a measuring cup and some kitchen scales too.

• Some of the recipes tell you to use a whisk. You can use an electric mixer, or a balloon whisk.

• To make some of the cakes, cookies, and sweets, you'll need to use the correct-sized cake pans or other special equipment. These items (and others that you may not have on hand) are listed at the start of each recipe.

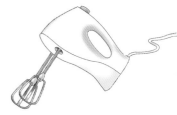

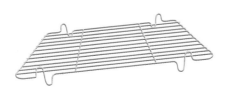

Safety and Hygiene

It is important to take care in the kitchen as there are lots of potential hazards and hygiene risks.

 Whenever you see the warning triangle you will need to supervise any child who is helping you.

- Before starting any cooking, always wash your hands.

- Cover any cuts with a bandage.

- Wear an apron to protect your clothes.

- Always make sure that all the equipment you use is clean.

- If a sharp knife is needed to cut up something hard, be sure to assist your young helpers. Always use a cutting board.

- Remember that trays in the oven and pans on the stove can get very hot. **Do not allow children to turn on the oven and to get things in and out of the oven for you.**

- Always assist children in using anything electrical – like an electric mixer.

- Be careful when heating anything in a pan on top of the stove. Keep the handle turned to one side to avoid accidentally knocking the pan off the stove.

- Keep your pets out of the kitchen while cooking.

Getting Started

Making your own cakes, cookies, and sweets is great fun and really quite easy. Best of all, everyone will enjoy what you create!

Measuring:

Use scales to weigh exactly how much of each ingredient you need, or use a measuring cup to measure liquids.

Mixing:

Use a spoon, balloon whisk, or electric hand mixer to combine the ingredients.

Different ideas:

Decorate your cakes and cookies with flavored or colored icing, and then add chocolate chips, sweets, or sprinkles.

Different shapes:

Cookie cutters come in lots of different shapes and sizes and can be bought from most supermarkets. If you don't have any cookie cutters of your own, carefully use a knife to cut out the shapes you want.

Creating recipes:

Once you've made a recipe in this book a few times, think about whether you could make your own version. Why not mix some chocolate chips into the Yuletide Bars mixture? This way you can start to make up your own recipes and write them at the back of this book. Try to think up names for the things you create!

Read through each recipe to make sure you've got all the ingredients that you need before you start.

Some recipes call for self-rising flour. if you do not have this in the house, you can make your own by mixing together 1 cup all-purpose flour, ½ teaspoon salt, and 1½ teaspoons baking powder.

Snowman Cupcakes

These cute cupcakes will brighten up any Christmas feast!

Snowman Cupcakes

Top Tip
Make your own snowman faces using ready-to-roll icing and food coloring.

You will need:

Extra equipment:
a cupcake pan
baking cups
a dessert decorator

Ingredients:
8 oz (225 g) self-rising flour
3 oz (80 g) butter
3 oz (80 g) superfine sugar
1 egg
3–4 fl. oz (80-100 ml) milk

For the topping:
8 oz (200 g) powdered sugar
4 oz (100 g) butter, softened
1 teaspoon vanilla extract
1 tablespoon milk
12 icing snowman head decorations
edible glitter

Preheat the oven to 350°F (180°C)

1 Put the baking cups in the cupcake pan.

2 Sift the flour into a bowl, followed by the butter. Use the tips of your fingers to rub the butter and flour together until the mixture becomes crumbly.

3 Add the sugar and mix it in, then stir in the egg. Finally, add enough milk to make the mixture creamy.

4 Put spoonfuls of the mixture into the baking cups. Bake for 10–15 minutes, until the cupcakes are golden brown; then leave them to cool on a wire rack.

5 Sift the powdered sugar into a bowl and then add the butter, vanilla extract, and a tablespoon of milk. Mix well. Then place the mixture into a dessert decorator.

6 Dispense the topping onto the cooked cupcakes. Top with an icing snowman head and sprinkle with edible glitter.

Candy Canes

These cool candy canes look great hanging on the Christmas tree!

Candy Canes

1 Whisk the butter and sugar in a bowl, beat in the vanilla extract and the egg, and then add the flour. Beat until smooth, and separate the mixture into two.

2 Blend one half of the mixture with red food coloring, adding drops until you get the depth of color you want. Wrap both mixtures in plastic wrap and place them in the refrigerator to chill for 30 minutes.

3 Roll both of the doughs out until they are 1/4 inch (5 mm) thick. Cut the dough into 1/5 inch (1/2 cm) strips and chill for 5–10 minutes until slightly firm.

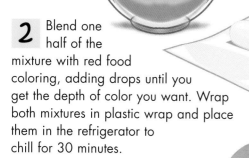

You will need:

Extra equipment:
plastic wrap
a rolling pin
a baking sheet
parchment paper
a spatula

Ingredients:
7 oz (200 g) butter
5 oz (150 g) superfine sugar
2 teaspoons vanilla extract
1 egg
10 oz (300 g) flour, sifted
red food coloring

Preheat the oven to
350°F (180°C)

Top Tip
Decorate your tree with these canes or wrap and give as gifts!

4 Take one strip of each color, and press on top of the other. Twist the strips together to make a candy cane, pinching the ends. Repeat until all of the strips have been used.

5 Place onto a baking sheet lined with parchment paper. Chill for 10 minutes, and then put them in the oven to bake for 8 minutes. Use a spatula to transfer the candy canes onto a wire rack to cool.

10

Christmas Tree Cookies

These pretty cookies make lovely decorations
– if they don't get eaten first!

Christmas Tree Cookies

1 Cream the butter and sugar together in a bowl until light and fluffy. Add the egg and mix well.

2 Sift the flour into the creamed mixture and, using your hands, create a smooth, firm dough. Refrigerate the mixture for 15 minutes.

3 Roll the dough out on a floured surface until it is 1/2 inch (5 mm) thick. Using cookie cutters or a sharp knife, cut out tree shapes and place on a greased baking sheet. Use a skewer to make holes at the top of each cookie. Bake for 10 minutes or until golden brown. Leave to cool on a wire rack.

4 For the icing, sift the powdered sugar into a bowl. Add the water and mix to form a smooth, thick paste. Halve the icing into two bowls. Add green food coloring to one bowl, then divide up the rest of the icing for the pale green, red, black, and white colors.

You will need:

Extra equipment:
a rolling pin
cookie cutters or a knife
a baking sheet, a knife
a dessert decorator
thin ribbon
a skewer

Ingredients:
4 oz (100 g) butter
4 oz (100 g) superfine sugar
1 egg
8 oz (225 g) flour

To decorate:
4 oz (100 g) powdered sugar
1–2 tablespoons water
green, red, and black food coloring

Preheat the oven to 350°F (180°C)

Top Tip
Remember to wash the dessert decorator before adding the next color!

5 Spread green icing over the cookies with a palette knife. Transfer the different colored icings to the dessert decorator and apply the finer details. Finish by tying on the ribbon.

Sweetie Cookies

These clever cookies will make your Christmas tree look really special!

Sweetie Cookies

1 Use a paper towel to grease the baking sheet with a little butter. Sift the flour and ground cinnamon into a bowl.

You will need:

Extra equipment:
a baking sheet
plastic wrap
a rolling pin
a clean plastic bag
a skewer
cookie cutters
several yards of fine ribbon
or silver thread

Ingredients:
8 oz (225 g) flour
1/2 teaspoon ground cinnamon
4 oz (100 g) butter
4 oz (100 g) superfine sugar
1 tablespoon milk
10 colored hard candies

Preheat the oven to 350°F (180°C)

3 Add the sugar and milk to the bowl, and knead the mixture into a soft dough. Wrap the dough in plastic wrap and put it in the fridge for 15 minutes.

2 Cut the butter into small pieces. Add it to the flour, and rub the mixture through your fingertips until it looks crumbly.

4 Put the dough onto a floured surface and roll it out. Use cookie cutters to cut out different shapes and put them on the baking sheet.

5 Put the hard candies in a plastic bag and crush them with a rolling pin. Carefully cut out a small hole from the center of each cookie. Fill the holes with the crushed sweets. Use the skewer to pierce a hole in the top of each cookie.

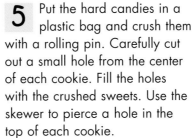

6 Bake the cookies for 10–15 minutes, until they are golden brown and the sweets have melted. Remove from oven. Once the melted sweets have set, carefully lift the cookies onto a wire rack to cool.

7 Thread the hole at the top of each cookie with ribbon or thread and hang them on your Christmas tree!

Snowball Cupcakes

These cupcakes are so tiny you will have plenty to share!

Snowball Cupcakes

You will need:
Extra equipment:
baking cups

Ingredients:
8 oz (225 g) white chocolate
1 oz (25 g) butter
8 oz (225 g) chunky fruit
and nut mix

1 Either use a double-boiler or put a heat-proof bowl over a saucepan of just simmering water. Make sure the bowl doesn't touch the water. Break the chocolate into small pieces and put it into the bowl or the top of the double-boiler with the butter. Stir the ingredients gently over low heat until they have melted.

Top Tip
These little cupcakes taste just as good made with milk chocolate!

3 Spoon a little of the mixture into each baking cup. Leave the snowball cupcakes in a cool place to set.

2 Take the pan off the burner, and take the bowl or the top of the double-boiler off the pan. Add the fruit and nut mix to the bowl and stir it into the chocolate mixture until it is thoroughly coated.

 # Christmas Truffles

A box of these chocolate truffles makes the perfect present!

Christmas Truffles

You will need:

Extra equipment:
a plastic container
baking cups

Ingredients:
6 oz (150 g) plain chocolate
5 fl oz (150 ml) heavy cream
1 oz (25 g) butter

To coat the truffles:
cocoa powder

1 Use a double-boiler or put a heat-proof bowl over a saucepan of just-simmering water. Make sure the bowl doesn't touch the water. Break the chocolate into small pieces and put them into the bowl, or the top of the double-boiler, and then add the cream and butter. Stir the mixture until the chocolate has melted.

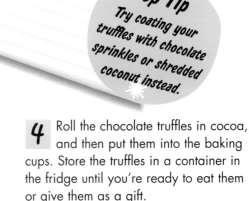

Top Tip
Try coating your truffles with chocolate sprinkles or shredded coconut instead.

2 Take the saucepan off the heat. Take the bowl off the saucepan and let it cool for a few minutes. Carefully pour the melted chocolate into the container. Put the lid on the container and leave it in the fridge to set for 3–4 hours.

3 Remove the container from the fridge. Roll small balls of the chocolate mixture in your hands.

4 Roll the chocolate truffles in cocoa, and then put them into the baking cups. Store the truffles in a container in the fridge until you're ready to eat them or give them as a gift.

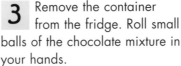
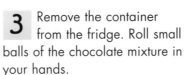

19

White Festive Fudge

This delicious fudge will be eaten up in no time!

White Festive Fudge

You will need:

Extra equipment:
a square baking pan 6 in. (15 cm)
wax paper

Ingredients:
10 oz (300 g) white chocolate
7 fl. oz (200 ml) sweetened condensed milk
2 teaspoons vanilla extract
3 oz (90 g) dried cranberries, chopped

1 Line the tin with wax paper.

2 Put the chocolate, condensed milk, and vanilla extract into a saucepan over medium heat. Stir them together until the chocolate has melted.

3 Add the chopped dried cranberries and mix well.

4 Pour the mixture into the pan and smooth the top with the back of a metal spoon. Put the pan into the fridge for 3–4 hours.

5 Remove the fudge from the pan by lifting it with the wax paper. Turn it over onto a cutting board and peel off the paper. Cut the slab of fudge into squares.

Top Tip
Tie with ribbons or put into paper boxes for pretty gifts!

Jelly Delight

This delight is sweet and juicy to eat!

Jelly Delight

1 Prepare the gelatin following the packet instructions. Stir the contents of the gelatin packet in boiling water with a wooden spoon until it has dissolved. Pour the gelatin into the dish and put it in the fridge to set.

You will need:

Extra equipment:
a small square dish

Ingredients:
5 oz (135 g) packet of strawberry, raspberry, or orange gelatin

To decorate:
powdered sugar

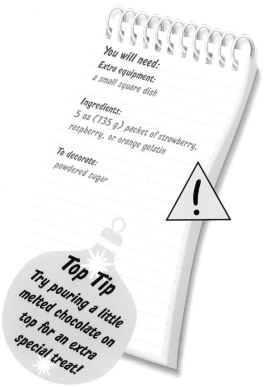

Top Tip
Try pouring a little melted chocolate on top for an extra special treat!

2 When the gelatin has set, loosen the edges from the dish and cut it into squares.

3 Carefully turn the gelatin over onto a plate or board covered in powdered sugar. Turn the squares of gelatin until they are completely covered.

Easy Christmas Cake

Make this festive treat for your whole family to enjoy!

Easy Christmas Cake

You will need:
Extra equipment:
a loaf pan 8 x 5 in. (20 x 13 cm)

Ingredients:
4 oz (100 g) margarine
1 large egg
1 tablespoon pear and apple jam
or thick honey
6 oz (150 g) self-rising
whole wheat flour
8 oz (225 g) mincemeat
orange juice

To decorate:
4 oz (100 g) powdered sugar
1-2 tablespoons orange juice

Preheat the oven to 325°F (160°C)

Top Tip
Tie a wide ribbon around your cake and add festive decorations.

1 Grease the loaf pan with a little margarine. Put the margarine, egg, and pear and apple jam (or honey) in a bowl and mix them together until they're light and creamy.

2 Sift the flour into the bowl and mix it in gently. Add the mincemeat and mix well. Then add enough orange juice to make a soft mixture.

3 Put the mixture into the pan, smoothing the top with the spoon. Bake for 40 minutes, until it is golden brown.

4 Leave the cake in the pan for 5 minutes, and then turn it over onto a wire rack to cool.

5 Sift the powdered sugar into a bowl, and mix in enough orange juice to make a thick paste. Spoon the mixture over the cake, letting it run down the sides.

Gingerbread Faces

These Santa and Rudolph faces are sure to be a hit!

Gingerbread Faces

1 Put the sugar, syrup, molasses, cinnamon, ginger, ground cloves, and a tiny bit of water into a pan.

3 Turn off the heat, then stir in the butter, baking soda, and flour until you have a smooth dough.

2 Heat up the mixture, stirring the whole time with a wooden spoon, until it is bubbling hard.

4 Wrap the dough in a piece of plastic wrap and leave it in the fridge for 30 minutes.

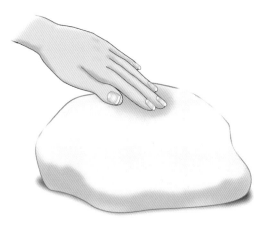

5 Place the dough onto a sheet of wax paper, then put another sheet on top. Using a rolling pin, roll the dough flat between the sheets until it is $1/8$ inch (3 mm) thick.

6 Using a cookie cutter or a sharp knife, cut out cookies from the flat dough. Place the shapes onto a baking sheet covered with a sheet of wax paper.

7 Bake the cookies for 10–15 minutes, until they are firm. Remove the hot baking sheet from the oven. Use a spatula to transfer the cookies to a wire rack to cool. Once cool, decorate with royal icing.

8 To make royal icing, beat the egg white in a small bowl, then sift in the powdered sugar. Beat the mixture until the icing becomes smooth and thick. Add a few drops of food coloring for the different face details. Spoon the icing into a dessert decorator and carefully apply your decoration onto the gingerbread. Leave the icing to set.

Snowball Cakes

These snowballs are much too tasty for throwing!

Snowball Cakes

Take Note!
Help children to use the electric mixer.

You will need:

Extra equipment:
a baking sheet
wax paper
baking cups

Ingredients:
2 1/2 oz (75 g) powdered sugar
8 oz (225 g) butter, softened
2 teaspoons vanilla extract
9 oz (250 g) flour
3 oz (90 g) nuts, pecans or almonds, finely chopped
1/2 teaspoon salt

To decorate:
powdered sugar

Preheat the oven to 325°F (170°C)

1 With a wooden spoon or electric mixer, mix the powdered sugar, butter, and vanilla extract together in a mixing bowl until you have a smooth paste.

2 Add the flour, nuts, and salt to the mixture and stir. Keep mixing until all the ingredients are combined and you have a smooth dough.

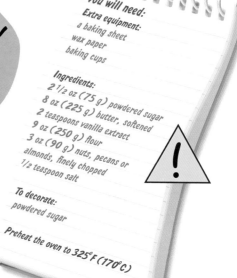

3 Using a teaspoon, spoon dollops of the dough onto a baking sheet lined with wax paper.

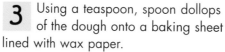

4 Bake the snowball cakes for 15–20 minutes. They should be just golden, so make sure you don't overcook them!

5 Remove the hot baking sheet from the oven. Roll the snowball cakes across a plate of powdered sugar before they cool completely.

6 Leave the decorated snowball cakes on a wire rack to cool. Serve them in baking cups with an extra dusting of powdered sugar for a really snowy finish!

Shortbread Snowmen

The sugar on these crunchy snowmen glistens like frost!

Shortbread Snowmen

1 Put the butter and sugar into a mixing bowl. Using a wooden spoon, mix them together until they make a smooth paste.

2 Sift the flour into the bowl.

3 Add the semolina and then stir the mixture well.

Top Tip
You can use melted chocolate or icing to decorate your snowmen.

4 When it seems as if the mixture won't stir any more, use your hands to knead it. The dough will be ready when it is smooth and there are no pieces left on the sides of the bowl.

5 Place the mixture on top of a sheet of wax paper, then put another sheet on top. Using a rolling pin, roll the dough flat between the sheets until it is about 1/8 inch (3 mm) thick.

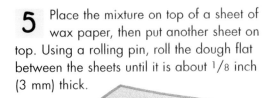

7 Bake the shortbread for 15–20 minutes. Remove the hot tray from the oven. Use a spatula to lift the snowmen onto a wire rack to cool.

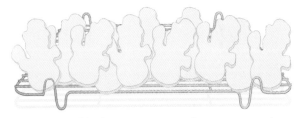

8 Sprinkle the snowmen with sugar to make them glisten. Why not make cool Santa shortbread cookies too and cover them with colored icing?

6 Use a snowman-shaped cookie cutter or a sharp knife to cut out shapes from the dough. Lay the shapes on a baking sheet lined with wax paper.

# Snowflakes

Try this simple recipe for some tasty chocolate treats!

Snowflakes

1 Use a double-boiler or put a heat-proof bowl over a saucepan of just-simmering water. Make sure the bowl doesn't touch the water. Break the chocolate into small pieces and put it into the bowl or the top of the double-boiler. Stir gently over low heat until the chocolate has melted.

You will need:
Extra equipment:
baking cups

Ingredients:
7 oz (200 g) white chocolate
4 oz (120 g) cornflakes

Top Tip
These little cakes taste just as good made with milk chocolate!

2 Stir the chocolate and the cornflakes together in a large mixing bowl.

3 Spoon the mixture into individual baking cups.

4 Leave the snowflakes in the fridge for 2 hours, or until the chocolate has set.

Hazelnut Candles

These crunchy candles look great decorated
with silver dragées and sweets!

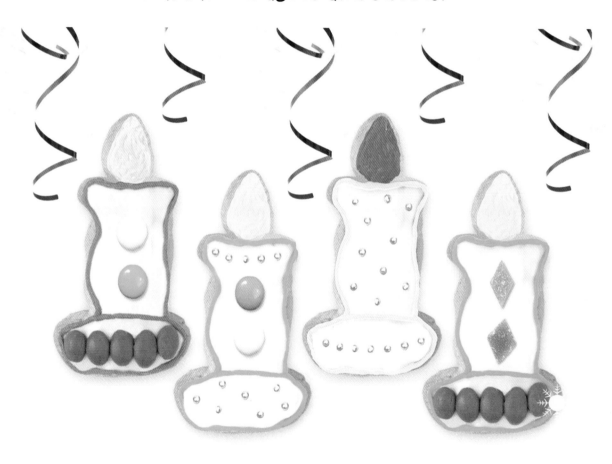

Hazelnut Candles

Top Tip
To soften the butter, take it out of the fridge at least 30 minutes before cooking.

You will need:

Extra equipment:
wax paper
a candle-shaped cookie cutter or knife
a baking sheet
a rolling pin

Ingredients:
4 oz (120 g) butter, softened
4 oz (120 g) sugar
1/2 teaspoon lemon juice
1 pinch cinnamon
1 pinch ground cloves
1 pinch nutmeg
8 oz (230 g) flour
3 1/2 oz (100 g) hazelnuts, ground
2 1/2 oz (75 g) powdered sugar
1 tablespoon water
silver dragées and sweets, to decorate

Preheat the oven to 400°F (200°C)

1 Mix the butter, sugar, lemon juice, cinnamon, ground cloves, nutmeg, flour, and hazelnuts together in a bowl with a wooden spoon until a smooth dough is made.

2 Place the mixture on top of a sheet of wax paper; then put another sheet on top. Using a rolling pin, roll the dough flat between the sheets until it is 1/4 inch (6 mm) thick.

3 Using a candle-shaped cookie cutter or a sharp knife, cut out cookies from the dough. Place them onto a baking sheet lined with wax paper.

4 Bake the cookies for 10–15 minutes, or until they are golden brown. Take the hot baking sheet from the oven. Use a spatula to transfer the cookies to a wire rack to cool.

5 Why not ice your hazelnut candles with a delicious sugar coating? Find out how to make icing on page 47. You could decorate your cookies with pretty silver dragées and sweets if you like!

37

Christmas Macaroons

 Perfect while you wait for Christmas dinner!

Christmas Macaroons

Take Note!
Ask an adult to help you use the electric mixer.

You will need:
Extra equipment:
a baking sheet
wax paper

Ingredients:
2 egg whites
1/2 teaspoon lemon juice
a pinch of salt
5 oz (150 g) powdered sugar
1/2 teaspoon cinnamon
5 oz (150 g) shredded coconut

Preheat the oven to 300°F (150°C)

1 Whisk the egg whites in a mixing bowl until they form soft peaks.

2 Continue whisking while adding the lemon juice, salt, powdered sugar, and cinnamon a little at a time. Be careful not to whisk too much, though, or the mixture will go soft. Now fold in the coconut.

3 Using a tablespoon, scoop dollops of the mixture onto a baking sheet lined with wax paper. Make sure you leave spaces between the dollops as they will expand during cooking!

4 Cook the macaroons for 25–30 minutes. When they are done, remove the hot baking sheet from the oven. Use a spatula to transfer the macaroons to a wire rack to cool.

Yuletide Log

This cake makes a perfect treat!

Yuletide Log

You will need:
Extra equipment:
a swiss roll tin
9 x 12 in. (22.5 x 30 cm)
wax paper

Ingredients:
margarine to grease
3 large eggs
3 oz (75 g) superfine sugar
2 oz (50 g) self-rising flour
1 oz (25 g) cocoa powder
For the filling and the top:
5 oz (150 g) dark chocolate
3 oz (80 g) unsalted butter
10 1/2 oz (300 g) powdered sugar, sifted
2 3/4 fl. oz (75 ml) whole milk

Preheat the oven to 400°F (200°C)

1 Put the tin on a sheet of wax paper and draw around it, leaving an edge of 1 in. (2.5 cm). Cut out the paper shape and make a slit at each corner. Grease the tin with some soft margarine. Now fit the paper into the tin, folding in the edges. Finally, grease the paper.

2 Break the eggs into a large bowl. Add the sugar, and whisk for a few minutes until the mixture is very light and creamy.

3 Hold the sifter above the bowl and sift the flour and cocoa powder into the mixture. Use a tablespoon to stir in the flour, using a *gentle* figure-eight movement – you don't want to knock out the air you've just whisked in!

4 Put the mixture into the tin, and then smooth the top with the back of a tablespoon. Bake for 7–10 minutes, until the edges have shrunk slightly away from the tin. Leave the cake to cool in the tin for 1–2 minutes.

5 Lay out another sheet of wax paper and sprinkle superfine sugar all over it. While the cake is still warm, turn it over onto the paper. Trim off the edges with a knife.

6 For the icing, suspend a heat-proof bowl over a pan of simmering water, making sure the base of the bowl doesn't touch the water (or use a double-boiler). Add the chocolate and butter and stir until melted, glossy, and well combined. Add the powdered sugar and beat until well combined, then stir in the milk and set aside to cool.

7 Spread the cake with one-third of the chocolate icing in an even layer. Now roll the cake tightly, using the wax paper to help you.

8 Spread the remaining icing on top of the cake. Sprinkle some powdered sugar over the cake to finish.

Top Tip
Decorate your yule log with holly or Christmas cake decorations. Yule logs make a great Christmas cake alternative for chocolate lovers!

Winter Snow Cupcakes

 These cupcakes are ice-cool!

Winter Snow Cupcakes

You will need:

Extra equipment:
a cupcake pan
baking cups
a rolling pin

Ingredients:
3 eggs
5 oz (150 g) butter, softened
5 oz (150 g) sugar
6 oz (175 g) self-rising flour
1 teaspoon vanilla extract

For the topping:
ready-to-roll fondant icing
blue food coloring
icing snowflakes

Preheat the oven to 350°F (175°C)

Take Note!
Ask an adult to help you use the electric mixer.

1 Put the baking cups in the cupcake pan.

2 Crack the eggs into a bowl and beat lightly with a fork. Add the beaten eggs to a large bowl containing the butter, sugar, flour, and vanilla extract.

3 Beat with an electric mixer for 2 minutes, until the mixture is light and creamy.

4 Use a teaspoon to transfer equal amounts of the mixture to the baking cups. Bake the cupcakes for 18–20 minutes. Leave them to cool on a wire rack.

5 Knead a couple of drops of food coloring into half the fondant icing. When the color is even, roll out the icing and cut out snowflake shapes to cover each cupcake. Decorate with small white icing snowflakes.

Christmas Party Cakes

Use lots of brightly colored icing to decorate these fun cakes!

Christmas Party Cakes

You will need:

Extra equipment:
baking cups
a cupcake pan
a dessert decorator (optional)

Ingredients:
8 oz (225 g) self-rising flour
3 oz (75 g) margarine
3 oz (75 g) granulated sugar
1 egg
3-4 fl. oz (75-100 ml) milk

Turn to the next page to find out how
to make different-flavored cakes.

Preheat the oven to 400°F (200°C)

1 Put the baking cups in the cupcake pan. Sift the flour into a bowl.

2 Put the margarine in the bowl. Use the tips of your fingers to rub the margarine and flour together until the mixture becomes crumbly.

3 Add the sugar and mix it in. Now stir in the egg. Finally, add enough milk to make the mixture creamy.

4 Put spoonfuls of the mixture into the baking cups. Bake the cakes for 10–15 minutes, until they are golden brown; then leave them to cool on a wire rack.

To decorate:

for water icing:	for royal icing:
4 oz (100 g) powdered sugar	4 oz (100 g) powdered sugar
1-2 tablespoons of water	1 egg white
food coloring	food coloring

Decorating the Christmas Party Cakes

1 Cover the cakes with water icing. Here's how to make it! Sift the powdered sugar into a bowl. Add 1–2 tablespoons of hot water and mix until you have a smooth, thick paste. Add one or two drops of food coloring if you want colored icing.

To make chocolate icing, add one teaspoon of cocoa powder to the powdered sugar before sifting. To make lemon icing, add 1–2 tablespoons of lemon juice instead of hot water.

You can decorate your cakes with sugar sprinkles, silver dragées or sweets. Once the water icing has set, why not add royal icing decorations?

2 To make royal icing, beat an egg white in a small bowl. Sift the powdered sugar into the bowl. Beat the mixture until the icing becomes smooth and thick. Add a drop of food coloring if you wish. Spoon the icing into a dessert decorator and carefully apply your decoration onto the cakes.
Leave the icing to set.

Top Tip
Decorate your cakes with sugar sprinkles, silver dragées, or small sweets!

Variations

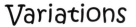

Chocolate Chip Party Cakes

Sift 1 oz (25 g) cocoa into the bowl with the flour. Mix in a handful of chocolate chips. When the cakes are cooked and cooled, cover them with chocolate water icing (see method above).

Coconut Party Cakes

Add 2 oz (50 g) dried coconut to the mixture with the sugar. When the cakes are cooked, top them with lemon water icing (see method above) and sprinkle them with more coconut.

Cherry Party Cakes

Add 4 oz (100 g) chopped glacé cherries to the mixture with the sugar. When the cakes are cooked, cover them with lemon water icing (see method above) and top each cake with half a glacé cherry.

Angel Cakes

These cakes may look fancy, but they're simple to make!

Angel Cakes

1 Put the baking cups in the cupcake pan.

You will need:

Extra equipment:
a cupcake pan
baking cups

Ingredients:
4 oz (100 g) butter, softened
4 oz (100 g) granulated sugar
2 eggs
4 oz (100 g) self-rising flour

For the buttercream icing:
3 oz (75 g) butter
6 oz (150 g) powdered sugar
1-2 tablespoons milk
food coloring (optional)

Preheat the oven to 375°F (190°C)

Top Tip
To soften the butter, take it out of the fridge at least 30 minutes before cooking.

2 Put the butter and sugar into a mixing bowl. Use a wooden spoon to beat them together until the mixture is fluffy and very pale in color.

4 Sift the rest of the flour into the bowl. Use a tablespoon to mix the ingredients gently, as if you were drawing a figure-eight. This will make sure your mixture stays nice and fluffy.

5 Use a teaspoon to transfer equal amounts of the mixture to the baking cups. Bake the cakes for 20–25 minutes, or until they are well risen and golden brown. Leave them to cool on a wire rack.

3 Beat in the eggs, one at a time, adding a tablespoon of flour with each one.

6 To make the angel wings, cut a slice from the top of each cake. Now cut each slice in half.

Take Note!
Ask an adult to help you use the electric mixer.

7 To make the buttercream icing, use a wooden spoon or an electric mixer to beat the butter in a large bowl until it is soft.

8 Sift half of the powdered sugar into the bowl, and then beat it with the butter until the mixture is smooth. Then sift the rest of the powdered sugar into the bowl and add one tablespoon of milk.

9 Beat the mixture until it is smooth and creamy. Now add a couple of drops of food coloring if you'd like.

10 If the mixture is too thick, add a little extra milk to make it more runny. Add extra powdered sugar if you need to thicken the mixture.

11 Place a little buttercream icing on top of each cupcake. Now gently push two of the halved slices into the icing on each cupcake at an angle to form pretty angel wings!

Cranberry Orange Muffins

Munch these tasty muffins as a snack with a drink!

Cranberry Orange Muffins

1 Put the baking cups in the muffin pan.

You will need:

Extra equipment:
a muffin pan
baking cups

Ingredients:
9 oz (250 g) flour
5 oz (150 g) sugar
1 tablespoon baking powder
1 egg
6 fl. oz (175 ml) milk
3 tablespoons vegetable oil
1 oz (80 g) chopped cranberries
2 tablespoons grated orange peel
2 tablespoons chopped pecans
or walnuts

Preheat the oven to 375°F (190°C)

Take Note!
Graters are sharp,
so watch your
fingers!

2 Sift the flour, sugar, and baking powder into a bowl. Mix them together.

4 Fold in the cranberries, orange peel, and nuts.

5 Use a teaspoon to transfer equal amounts of the mixture to the baking cups. Bake the muffins for 20 minutes, or until they are well risen and golden brown. Leave them to cool on a wire rack.

3 Add in the egg, milk, and vegetable oil, and mix until all the flour is moistened.

Christmas Spice Muffins

Put a little spice into Christmas!

Christmas Spice Muffins

1 Put the baking cups in the muffin pan.

You will need:
Extra equipment:
a muffin pan
baking cups
Ingredients:
4 oz (110 g) butter
5 oz (135 g) sugar
2 eggs
1/2 teaspoon ground cinnamon
1/2 teaspoon ground allspice
2 teaspoons baking powder
1/2 teaspoon baking soda
8 fl. oz (235 ml) applesauce
7 oz (190 g) flour
For the topping:
4 oz (120 g) powdered sugar
2 tablespoons water
nuts of your choice
Preheat the oven to 350°F (180°C)

2 In a large bowl mix together the butter and sugar until the mixture is creamy.

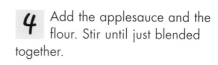

4 Add the applesauce and the flour. Stir until just blended together.

5 Use a teaspoon to divide the mixture equally into the muffin pan. Bake the muffins for 20 minutes.

3 Add in the eggs and beat until smooth. Blend in the cinnamon, allspice, baking powder, and baking soda.

6 When the muffins are cool, mix the powdered sugar and water and spoon a little icing over each one. Top with a few nuts.

Happy New Year Cake

Start the new year with this delicious cake!

Happy New Year Cake

1 Put the cake pan onto a sheet of wax paper and draw around it. Cut out the circle of paper. Use a paper towel to grease the pan with a little soft margarine, and then put the circle of wax paper inside the tin. Grease the paper.

You will need:

Extra equipment:
a round cake pan 9 in. (23 cm)
wax paper
a grater

Ingredients:
9 oz (250 g) butter
14 oz (400 g) granulated sugar
5 eggs, beaten
5 fl. oz (150 ml) sour cream
10 oz (300 g) flour
4 oz (100 g) cocoa powder
2 oz (50 g) ground almonds
1 teaspoon baking powder
1/2 teaspoon baking soda

Preheat the oven to 325°F (160°C)

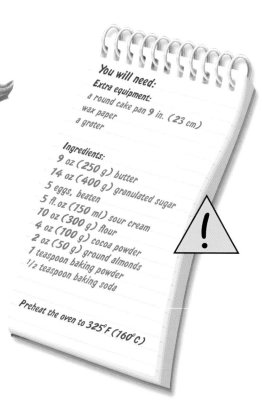

2 Cream the butter and sugar together until the mixture is pale and fluffy. Add the beaten eggs one at a time, mixing well; then add the sour cream.

To decorate:
4 oz (100 g) unsalted butter
7 oz (200 g) powdered sugar
4 tablespoons cocoa powder
drop of milk
3 oz (75 g) dark chocolate, grated

3 Sift the flour, cocoa powder, ground almonds, baking powder, and baking soda into the bowl. Fold them into the cake mixture gently.

4 Transfer the mixture to the cake pan and bake for about 90 minutes. Allow the cake to cool in the pan for ten minutes, then transfer it to a wire rack to cool completely.

Top Tip
Serve with whipped cream for an extra celebration treat!

Decorating the Cake

1 Before you start to decorate the cake, cut it into four layers, as shown.

2 To make the filling, place the butter in a bowl, then gradually sift and beat in the powdered sugar and cocoa powder, then enough milk to make the mixture fluffy. Refrigerate for 30 minutes before using.

3 Spread the filling onto the bottom layer of the cake and place the next layer on top. Continue, spreading the filling between each layer. Decorate the top and sides of the cake with the remaining filling.

4 Top with curls or shavings of dark chocolate.

Christmas Crunchers

Leave one for Santa and listen for the crunch!

Christmas Crunchers

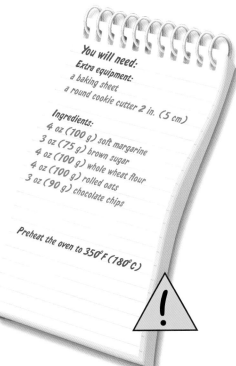

You will need:

Extra equipment:
a baking sheet
a round cookie cutter 2 in. (5 cm)

Ingredients:
4 oz (100 g) soft margarine
3 oz (75 g) brown sugar
4 oz (100 g) whole wheat flour
4 oz (100 g) rolled oats
3 oz (90 g) chocolate chips

Preheat the oven to 350°F (180°C)

1 Use a paper towel to grease the baking sheet with a little soft margarine. Put the margarine and sugar into a bowl and mix them together with a wooden spoon.

2 Add the flour, oats, and chocolate chips to the bowl. Mix everything together, using a spoon and then your hands, to make a soft dough.

3 Put the dough onto a floured surface and gently press it out.

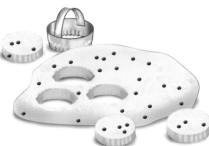

4 Cut out circles of dough and put them onto the baking sheet.

5 Bake the crunchers in the oven for 12–15 minutes, until they are golden brown. Place the cookies onto a wire rack to cool.

Peppermint Creams

These icy mints will give a cool Christmas kick!

Peppermint Creams

1 Sift the powdered sugar into a bowl.

You will need:
Extra equipment:
none

Ingredients:
1 lb (450 g) powdered sugar
1 pasteurized egg white
a few drops of peppermint extract
food coloring (optional)

For chocolate peppermint creams:
4 oz (100 g) plain chocolate, melted

2 Whisk the egg white in a bowl until it's frothy; then add it to the powdered sugar with a few drops of peppermint extract. Mix it together with the wooden spoon to make a very thick paste. Knead the paste with your hands until it is very smooth.

3 To make colored peppermint creams, put some of the mixture into another bowl and add one or two drops of food coloring. Mix it well. Do this for every different color used.

Top Tip
Use food coloring to make different-colored peppermint creams.

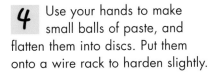

4 Use your hands to make small balls of paste, and flatten them into discs. Put them onto a wire rack to harden slightly.

5 You could dip your peppermint creams into melted chocolate. Leave them to set on the wire rack.

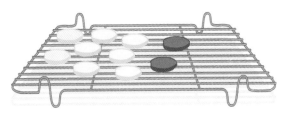

Carrot Muffins

Rudolph loves these muffins – they help him see in the dark!

Carrot Muffins

You will need:

Extra equipment:
a muffin pan
baking cups

Ingredients:
4 1/2 oz (125 g) whole wheat flour
4 1/2 oz (125 g) plain flour
4 oz (100 g) raisins
2 oz (60 g) brown sugar
1 teaspoon baking powder
8 fl. oz (225 ml) milk
4 oz (100 g) shredded carrots
2 eggs
2 oz (55 g) butter, melted

Preheat the oven to 375°F (190°C)

1 Put the baking cups in the muffin pan.

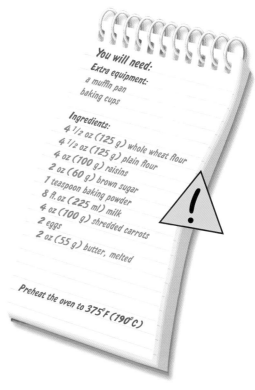

2 In a large bowl put the whole wheat flour, plain flour, raisins, sugar, and baking powder. Stir them all together with a wooden spoon until they are well mixed.

3 Put the remaining ingredients in a small bowl and mix together. Then add to the larger bowl and mix together.

4 Use a teaspoon to divide the mixture equally into the muffin pan. Bake the muffins for 20 minutes.

5 Leave the muffins in the pan until they are cool, and then remove them and enjoy.

Wild Berry Muffins

Your friends will go wild for these fruity Christmas treats!

Wild Berry Muffins

1 Put the baking cups in the muffin pan.

You will need:
Extra equipment:
a muffin pan
baking cups

Ingredients:
9 oz (250 g) flour
5 oz (150 g) sugar
2 1/2 teaspoons baking powder
1/4 teaspoon baking soda
8 fl. oz (240 ml) milk
4 fl. oz (115 ml) vegetable oil
2 eggs
7 oz (190 g) fresh berries

Preheat the oven to 400°F (200°C)

!

Take Note! Ask an adult to help you use the electric mixer.

2 Sift the flour, sugar, baking powder, and baking soda in a large bowl. Mix them together.

3 In another bowl, mix the milk, oil, and eggs. Add to the dry ingredients and mix well until just blended.

4 Fold the berries into the mixture.

5 Use a teaspoon to divide the mixture equally into the muffin pan. Bake the muffins for 15–20 minutes or until golden brown.

6 Loosen the edges and turn over onto a wire rack to cool.

Christmas Muffins

The perfect chocolaty treat!

Christmas Muffins

1 Put the baking cups in the muffin pan.

You will need:

Extra equipment:
a muffin pan
baking cups

Ingredients:
2 oz (50 g) butter, softened
3 oz (75 g) brown sugar
1 egg
4 oz (100 g) flour
2 teaspoons baking powder
1 tablespoon cocoa powder
3 fl. oz (90 ml) milk

To decorate:
fresh whipped cream
chocolate snowflakes

Preheat the oven to 350°F (180°C)

Top Tip
To soften the butter, take it out of the fridge at least 30 minutes before cooking.

2 Put the butter, sugar, egg, and flour into a large mixing bowl. Stir them all together with a wooden spoon until they are well mixed.

3 Sift the baking powder and cocoa powder into the bowl. Add the milk. Mix them together.

4 Use a teaspoon to divide the mixture equally into the muffin pan. Bake the muffins for 10–15 minutes.

5 Leave the muffins in the tray until they are cool, and then decorate them with fresh whipped cream. Add a little chocolate snowflake to finish.

Variations for the Christmas Muffins

1 Put the baking cups in the muffin pan. Sift the flour into a bowl.

2 Put the margarine in the bowl. Use the tips of your fingers to rub the margarine and flour together until the mixture becomes crumbly.

3 Add the sugar and stir in the egg. Finally, add enough milk to make the mixture creamy.

4 Put spoonfuls of the mixture into the baking cups. Bake the muffins for 10–15 minutes; then leave them to cool on a wire rack.

5 Decorate them with a generous swirl of fresh whipped cream. Cover with coconut and add a white chocolate snowflake.

You will need:

Ingredients:
8 oz (225 g) self-rising flour
3 oz (75 g) margarine
3 oz (75 g) granulated sugar
1 egg
3–4 fl. oz (75–100 ml) milk

To decorate:
fresh whipped cream
shredded coconut with food coloring
white chocolate snowflakes

Christmas Crackle Cakes

Use cornflakes or crisped rice to make these little cakes crackle!

Christmas Crackle Cakes

You will need:

Extra equipment:
baking cups

Ingredients:
1 oz (25 g) sugar
1 oz (25 g) butter
2 tablespoons cocoa powder
1 tablespoon corn syrup or honey
1 oz (25 g) cornflakes

To decorate:
colored chocolate candies

1 Put the sugar, butter, cocoa powder, and golden syrup or honey into a pan over low heat. Stir until the ingredients have melted.

Top Tip
Use crisped rice instead of cornflakes if you prefer.

2 Stir the cornflakes into the mixture until they are completely coated.

3 Spoon a little of the mixture into each of the baking cups. Top each with a colored chocolate candy and leave them to set.

Yuletide Bars

These yummy bars are perfect to munch on during long journeys to visit friends!

Yuletide Bars

1 To make the date filling:
Place the dates and water in a saucepan and ask an adult to cook them over low heat, stirring occasionally, until the dates are soft and have absorbed most of the water (about 5–10 minutes). Remove from the heat and stir in the vanilla extract. Leave to cool and then place it in the food processor and puree until smooth. Set aside.

You will need:

Extra equipment:
a food processor
a baking pan 8 x 11 in. (20 x 28 cm)
parchment paper
plastic wrap

Ingredients:
14 oz (400 g) pitted dried dates
8 fl. oz (240 ml) water
1 teaspoon pure vanilla extract
7 oz (200 g) rolled oats
4 1/2 oz (130 g) flour
5 1/2 oz (160 g) light brown sugar
1/2 teaspoon baking soda
1/4 teaspoon salt
1/8 teaspoon ground cinnamon
8 oz (225 g) butter, cut into cubes
Preheat the oven to 350°F (180°C)

2 Butter the baking pan and line the bottom with parchment paper.

3 To make the oaty crust: Place the oats, flour, sugar, baking soda, salt, and ground cinnamon in a bowl and mix together. Then add the butter and combine together until the mixture is crumbly. Press two-thirds of the mixture into the base of the prepared baking pan.

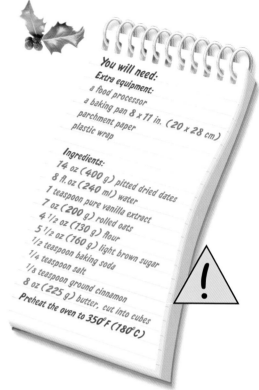

4 Spread the date mixture evenly over the oaty crust and then sprinkle the remaining oats evenly over the top of the dates. Bake for about 30–40 minutes or until golden brown. Place on a wire rack to cool. Once it has cooled, cover the pan with plastic wrap, and place in the refrigerator for at least one hour or until firm enough to cut easily into squares.

Coconut Ice

These simple sweets can be made in any colors you like!

Coconut Ice

1 Put the pan on the wax paper and draw around it. Cut out the square of paper large enough to overlap the sides; slit the corners and put it into the pan.

You will need:

Extra equipment:
a square baking pan 7 in. (18 cm)
wax paper

Ingredients:
2 lb (900 g) superfine sugar
1 oz (25 g) butter
1/4 pt (150 ml) milk
8 oz (225 g) shredded coconut
food coloring

Top Tip
Why not make green and white coconut ice?

2 Put the sugar, butter, and milk into a pot over medium heat, and bring the mixture to a boil. Let the mixture simmer for 4 minutes, stirring constantly.

5 Color the other half of the mixture with a few drops of food coloring. Pour it on top of the mixture in the pan and leave it to set. Cut the coconut ice into squares, but be careful – it will be very crumbly!

4 Pour half the mixture into the pan. Leave it to cool a little.

3 Remove the pot from the heat and stir in the coconut.

Santa Sweets

Make Santa's favorite sweets – they are delicious!

Santa Sweets

1 Put the almonds, sugar, and a little orange juice in a bowl. Mix them together to form a stiff paste.

You will need:

Extra equipment:
a toothpick
wax paper

Ingredients:
6 oz (150 g) ground almonds
4 oz (100 g) superfine sugar
1-2 tablespoons orange juice

To decorate:
powdered sugar

For chocolate almond sweets:
cocoa powder or
2 oz (50 g) plain chocolate, melted

2 Use your hands to roll the paste into small balls. To decorate, put a little powdered sugar on a plate, and roll the balls around in it until they are evenly coated.

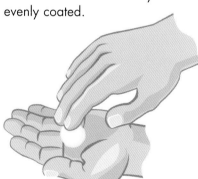

3 For chocolate almond sweets, you can either roll the balls in cocoa powder or cover them with melted chocolate. Use a toothpick to dip the almond sweets into the melted chocolate, and then leave them on a piece of wax paper to set.

Holiday Honeycomb

Coat honeycomb in melted chocolate or just eat it as is!

Holiday Honeycomb

You will need:

Extra equipment:
a square baking pan 7 in. (18 cm)

Ingredients:
a little butter
5 tablespoons granulated sugar
2 tablespoons corn syrup
1 teaspoon baking soda

For chocolate honeycomb:
2 oz (50 g) milk chocolate, melted

Warning! The honeycomb mixture will be extremely hot!

1 Use a paper towel to grease the baking pan with a little butter. Put the sugar and syrup into a saucepan over medium heat. Bring the mixture to a boil, then let it simmer for about 3–4 minutes until it becomes golden brown.

2 Take the saucepan off the heat, add the baking soda, and mix it in with a wooden spoon. When the mixture froths up, pour it into the baking pan right away.

3 When the mixture has cooled, turn it over onto a cutting board and use the wooden spoon to crack it into bite-sized pieces.

4 You can dip pieces of honeycomb into melted chocolate if you'd like! Leave them to cool on a piece of wax paper.

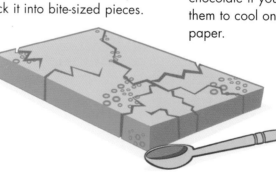

Chocolate Fridge Cake

This chocolate treat is great to take on an outing!

Chocolate Fridge Cake

1 Use a paper towel to grease the pan with a little butter. Put some water in a saucepan and warm it over low heat. Put the butter, chocolate, and corn syrup into a heat-proof bowl. Stand the bowl over the pan, stirring the ingredients until they have melted.

You will need:

Extra equipment:
a square pan 7 in. (18 cm)
a clean plastic bag
a rolling pin

Ingredients:
3 oz (75 g) butter
3 oz (75 g) plain chocolate
2 tablespoons corn syrup
6 oz (175 g) graham crackers
3 oz (75 g) raisins
1 oz (25 g) shredded coconut
2 oz (50 g) chopped nuts

To decorate:
1 oz (25 g) plain chocolate
colored chocolate candies

Top Tip
Dip a spoon in hot water before measuring the syrup – the heat makes the syrup slide off the spoon!

2 Put the graham crackers into a clean plastic bag and crush them with a rolling pin.

3 Take the bowl off the pan and add the graham crackers, raisins, coconut, and chopped nuts, mixing everything together thoroughly. Put the mixture into the pan, pressing it down firmly.

4 To decorate, melt the chocolate in a clean bowl over a pan of simmering water, as before. Spread the chocolate evenly over the mixture in the pan. Mark nine squares in the chocolate fridge cake, and then put the chocolate candies on top. Leave it to set in a cool place for 2–3 hours, and then cut it into squares.

Christmas Toffee Pudding

Try this sticky dessert instead of traditional Christmas pudding!

Christmas Toffee Pudding

To make the pudding:

1 Soak the dates in boiling water, then allow them to cool. Add baking soda and mix in a food processor.

2 Cream the butter and sugar together, and beat in the egg. Carefully fold in both flours and mix in the cooled date mixture to form a sloppy dough.

3 Pour the mixture into a medium, well-buttered pudding basin and cover the top with silver foil. Seal the edges and place in a preheated oven for approximately 30–40 minutes or until firm to the touch.

You will need:

Extra equipment:
a heat-proof oven bowl

Ingredients:

For the pudding:
3 oz (90 g) dried dates (pits removed)
1/5 pt (100 ml) boiling water
1/2 tsp baking soda
1 1/2 oz (45 g) unsalted butter
2 1/2 oz (75 g) superfine sugar
1 medium egg
1 1/2 oz (45 g) flour
1 1/2 oz (45 g) self-rising flour

For the toffee sauce:
3 1/2 oz (105 g) brown sugar
2 oz (60 g) butter
2 1/2 fl. oz (75 ml) heavy cream
vanilla extract

Preheat the oven to 350°F (180°C)

To make the toffee sauce:

1 Mix all the ingredients together in a small, thick-bottomed saucepan and heat until simmering.

2 Cook until toffee-colored.

Warning! The toffee sauce mixture will be extremely hot!

To serve:

1 Tip the pudding into a deep-sided, heat-proof dish and pour hot toffee sauce over it.

2 Place the dish under the broiler for a few seconds to allow the toffee sauce to bubble.

3 Serve with whipped cream or vanilla ice cream.

Festive Fritters

These tasty little nibbles are sure to make your party a big hit!

Festive Fritters

Take Note!
Ask an adult to help you use the deep fryer.

You will need:

Extra equipment:
plastic wrap
a gravy boat
a deep fryer

Ingredients:
4 oz (120 g) flour
5 fl. oz (150 ml) milk
1 fl. oz (30 ml) oil
1 pinch of salt
1 fl. oz (30 ml) egg white from approx. 2 eggs
16 canned apricot halves in natural juice
granulated sugar, to decorate

For the apricot sauce:
2 oz (60 g) powdered sugar
small jar of apricot jam

Preheat the fryer to 350°F (180°C)

To make the batter:

1 Sift the flour into a bowl. Gradually beat in the milk to produce a smooth batter.

2 Stir in the oil and salt.

3 Cover with plastic wrap and allow the mixture to rest for at least 10 minutes.

4 When you are ready to start cooking, beat the egg white until stiff, and gently fold it into the batter.

To cook:

1 Pre-heat the deep fryer to approximately 350°F (180°C).

2 Dust the apricot halves with a little flour and dip them into the batter.

3 Lift them out with a fork and carefully place in the hot oil. Fry gently until the batter is golden and crisp. Lift out onto paper to drain.

4 Dust with superfine sugar and serve with hot apricot sauce, made by boiling the apricot jam with a little of the fruit juice and straining into a gravy boat.

Santa Snaps

A crunchy Christmas classic and one of Santa's favorites!

Santa Snaps

1 Melt the butter, sugar, and syrup in a small pot. Stir in the flour and ginger; then add the grated rind of half a lemon and 1 tablespoon of the juice.

You will need:
Extra equipment:
a baking sheet
wax paper

Ingredients:
2 oz (60 g) butter
2 oz (60 g) superfine sugar
2 oz (60 g) corn syrup
2 oz (60 g) flour
1/2 teaspoon ground ginger
half a lemon

For the filling:
1/2 pt (300 ml) heavy cream
1/2 oz (15 g) powdered sugar
8 1/2 oz (240 g) fresh fruit

Preheat the oven to 350°F (180°C)

Take Note! Graters are sharp. Ask an adult to help you.

2 Place twelve tablespoons of the mixture (well spaced) on wax paper and press them down. Bake them for 8–10 minutes until golden brown. Allow to cool slightly, and then slide off the paper onto a wire rack.

3 Whip the cream with the powdered sugar until it forms soft peaks.

4 Spoon the fresh whipped cream into the middle of one snap, surround with fresh fruit, and sandwich with a second snap. Repeat with a third, and decorate the top with whipped cream and fruit.

5 Repeat the process to produce three more Santa snaps.

Mincemeat Parcels

Try this party version of the traditional treat – delicious dipped in cream!

Mincemeat Parcels

You will need:
Extra equipment:
a baking sheet

Ingredients:
4 sheets of ready-prepared filo dough
2 oz (60 g) butter (melted)
4 oz (120 g) mincemeat
1 egg yolk

Preheat the oven to 400°F (200°C)

Take Note!
Ask an adult to help you melt the butter.

1 Take one sheet of filo dough and brush with a little melted butter. Fold in half to sandwich the butter, cut this folded sheet in half, and again to form four equal quarters. Carefully butter the top of one quarter.

2 Place a second quarter on top at a slight angle, butter this, and repeat the process with a third and fourth square – you should have a filo star shape.

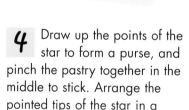

3 Place a spoonful of mincemeat in the center, and brush around the mincemeat with egg yolk whisked with a little water.

4 Draw up the points of the star to form a purse, and pinch the pastry together in the middle to stick. Arrange the pointed tips of the star in a decorative fashion.

Use the picture on page 87 as a guide for the final shape you need to achieve when shaping the pastry.

5 Brush the parcels with melted butter and bake for 10–15 minutes, or until golden and crisp.

6 Allow to cool slightly before serving. For a more festive look, dust them with powdered sugar and serve with whipped cream or vanilla ice cream.

Mincemeat Pies

Christmas wouldn't be complete without a hot mincemeat pie!

Mincemeat Pies

Top Tip
To soften the butter, take it out of the fridge at least 30 minutes before cooking.

You will need:

Extra equipment:
a cupcake pan
2 pastry cutters, one large and one medium

Ingredients:
8 oz (200 g) butter, softened
1 lb (450 g) flour
2 oz (50 g) powdered sugar
2 egg yolks
3–4 tablespoons iced water
1 lb (450 g) mincemeat
beaten egg, to glaze
superfine sugar, to decorate

Preheat the oven to 400°F (200°C)

1 Cut the butter into cubes. Sift the flour into a mixing bowl. Add the butter and, using your fingertips, rub the butter into the flour until it resembles fine breadcrumbs.

2 Stir in the powdered sugar. Make a well in the center, then stir in the egg yolk and about 3–4 tablespoons of iced water to make a soft, but not sticky, dough.

3 Knead lightly to form a smooth dough, and chill for 30 minutes.

4 On a floured surface, roll out two-thirds of the dough and cut out 30 rounds using the large pastry cutter. Use these to line the cupcake pan. Fill with mincemeat.

5 Re-roll the remaining pastry and trimmings and cut out circles using the medium cutter. Dampen the edges of each circle and place onto the pies. Use the trimmings to decorate the top of each pie.

6 Seal the edges, brush the tops with beaten egg, and cook for about 20 minutes or until they are golden brown. Transfer the mincemeat pies to a wire rack to cool. Dust with sugar to serve.

Your Recipes

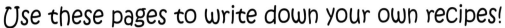

Use these pages to write down your own recipes!

 # Your Recipes

 # Your Recipes

# Your Recipes

 # Your Recipes

 # Your Recipes